For Him all Stars

15 CAROLS FOR UPPER VOICES

MUSIC DEPARTMENT

OXFORD

UNIVERSITY PRESS

OXFORD
UNIVERSITY PRESS

Great Clarendon Street, Oxford OX2 6DP, England
198 Madison Avenue, New York, NY,10016, USA

Oxford University Press is a department of the University of Oxford.
It furthers the University's aim of excellence in research, scholarship,
and education by publishing worldwide

Oxford is a registered trade mark of Oxford University Press
in the UK and in certain other countries

3 5 7 9 10 8 6 4 2

ISBN 978-0-19-335569-9

Music and text origination by
Barnes Music Engraving Ltd., East Sussex
Printed in Great Britain on acid-free paper by
Halstan & Co. Ltd., Amersham, Bucks.

Contents

in memoriam Susan Baldwin, 25 December 1986

1. Balulalow

Wedderburn, *Ane Compendious Bulk of*
Godly and Spiritual Sangis (Edinburgh, 1567)

ANTONY BALDWIN
(b. 1957)

* If using piano, the low F and C in bars 20 and 21 should be played up an octave (see cue notes).

heart,_____ and ne - ver, ne - ver mair from thee_ de - part.

2. But I shall praise_____ thee e - ver -

with sang - is sweet_____

- more_____ with sang - is sweet_ un - to_____ thy_

gloir,_____ the knees of my heart_____ shall__ I

bow,_____ and sing__ that richt_____ ba - lu - la -

- low._____

opt. solo 8' (different tone from bar 1)

soft 32'

7 March 1999

2. Ring the bells

Frances Jane Crosby (1820–1915)

ALAN BULLARD
(b. 1947)

with a song.

Wake your harps, ye

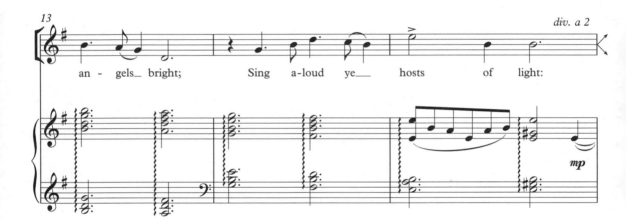

an - gels_ bright;   Sing a-loud ye_ hosts of light:

div. a 2

1. Sing as_ on that ho - ly_ night: Glo - ry in_ the

2. Sing,_ sing as_ on that ho - ly_ night: Glo - ry

and the sea,   Christ has___ come   our___

earth,   the sea,   Christ has___ come   our___

___ life   to be.   Wake your harps,   ye   an - gels___

___ life   to be.   Wake your harps,   ye

cresc.

Ped. ___

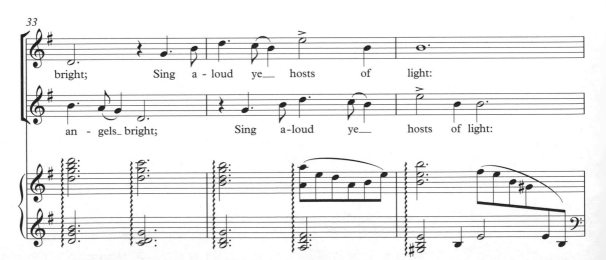

bright;   Sing   a - loud   ye___   hosts   of   light:

an - gels___ bright;   Sing   a - loud   ye___   hosts   of light:

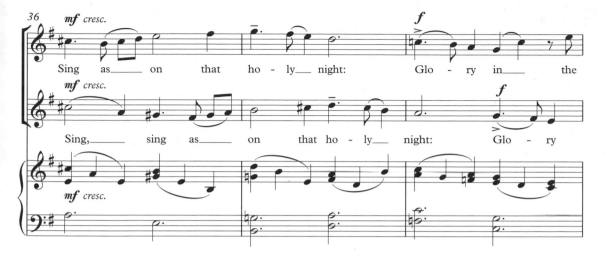

Lo, he comes with us to dwell: Christ the Lord Im-

Lo, he comes with us to dwell: Christ the Lord Im-

- man - u - el.

- man - u - el.

div. a 3

Ped.

1. Wake your harps, ye an - gels bright; Sing a-loud ye

2. Wake your harps, ye an - gels bright; Sing a-

3. Wake your harps, ye an - gels bright;

for Jan and Mary

3. Scots Nativity

Scottish trad.

ALAN BULLARD
(b. 1947)

This piece (T134) is available separately, and also in a version for SATB and piano (X446).

August 2001

bairn child;   *kine* cattle;   *Balow, lammy, baloobalow* Sleep, my little lamb

4. For him all stars have shone

Elizabeth Jennings

BOB CHILCOTT
(b. 1955)

The original version of this piece for upper-voice choir, SATB, and piano is available separately (BC57).

Text taken from 'The Shepherds' by Elizabeth Jennings; by permission of David Higham Associates. Music © Oxford University Press 2002 and 2006.

good-ness rules   the   earth.

He   is   so small   the

stars bow down_____   The fierce winds ease   their   breath,_____

5. We Three Camels

Jane Yolen

DAVID HAMILTON
(b. 1955)

14

oo_____

I car-ried a king, but not the One, through

I car-ried a king, but not the One,

17

oo_____   *oo_____*

sear-ing heat   and blind-ing sun, through nights so cold   my

through sear-ing heat and blind-ing sun,   through nights so cold,

6. Cradle Song

William Blake

CECILIA McDOWALL
(b. 1951)

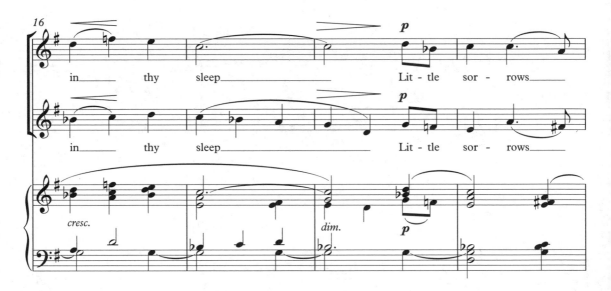

7. Vulcan

Words and music by
JENNY McLEOD
(b. 1941)

1. Peo-ple, look east, look you, The time is near.
2. We sing his ra - di-ance, We sing his shi - ning,
3. See him ce - les - ti - al, And know him ours,

1. The time is
2. We sing his
3. And know him

Rex Pacificus The King of Peace

Exultet coelum laudibus Let Heaven rejoice with praises;   *Agnoscat omne saeculum* Let every age and nation know

gloria tibi   glory to you

to Elizabeth

8. Tomorrow shall be my dancing day

English trad.
arr. MALCOLM PEARCE
(b. 1950)

A version of Malcolm Pearce's arrangement for SATB and organ is available separately (X461).

call my true love to my dance.   Sing

O my love,   O my love, my love, my love,   This

have I done for my true love.

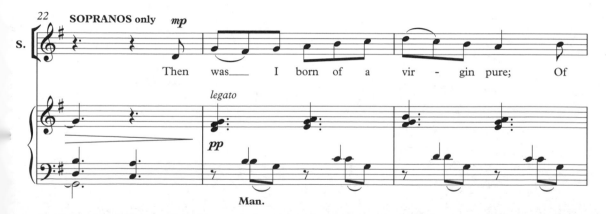

SOPRANOS only *mp*

Then was I born of a vir - gin pure;   Of

her___ I took___ flesh - ly___ sub-stance.   Thus   was   I   knit   to

man's_ na - ture,   To   call   my   true__ love to__ my   dance.

S.   Sing   O   my_ love,   O__ my   love,   my

A.   Sing   O   my   love,___   O__ my   love,   my

34 love, my love, This have I done for my— true love.

love, my love, sing O—————— for my true love.

37 *mp dolce*

mf ah——————

In a man - ger laid— and

p sempre legato

dim.

Ch. (Gt.) solo

41 ah——————

wrapp'd I was, So ve - ry poor— this was— my chance, Be -

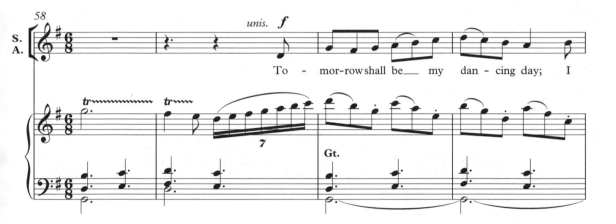

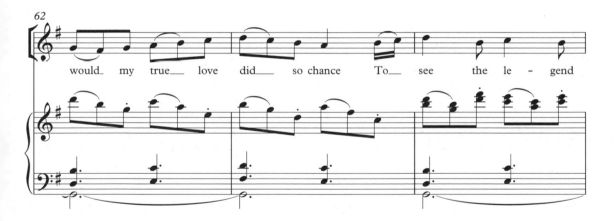

Sing O my love, O my love, my

love, my love, This have I done for my true love,

for my true love, for my true love,

for my true love.

9. Mary's Cradle Song

MAX REGER (1873–1916)
arr., with English text, by Paul Keene

This piece is available separately (W116).

* The alto part is optional, though desirable. If it is omitted, soprano 2 should sing the lowest part in bars 64–6.

sweet - ly now sings a bird____ up - on the bough:

'Sleep, ba - by, sleep, dear one,

sleep, Je - sus, sleep.'

espress.

S.1
2. Joy - ful is thy laugh - ter now, peace - ful is____ thy si - lent rest.

.2/A.
2. Joy - ful is thy laugh - ter now, and peace - ful is thy rest.

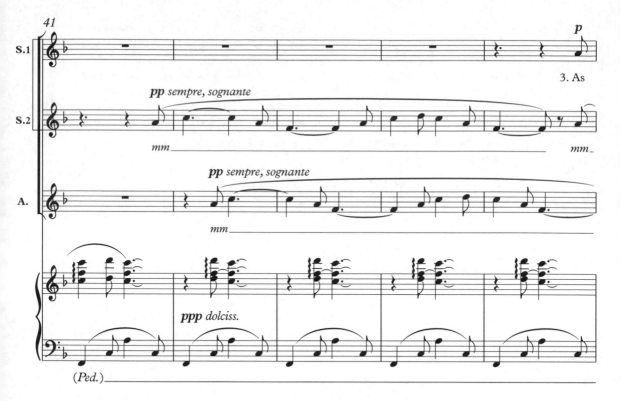

eve - ning falls the sun - light goes, the ro - ses now_ their pe - tals close.

Je - sus, lay thy head in rest sweet - ly on thy mo - ther's breast,

(mm) _____ mm _____

mm _____ mm _____

poco cresc.

dim.

Ped. _____

and through thy dreams will waft _ Ma - ry's cra - dle song so soft:

(pp)

mm _____

(pp)

mm _____

pp

Ped. _____

10. Love came down at Christmas

Christina Rossetti (1830–94)

JOHN RUTTER
(b. 1945)

This carol is also available in its original version, for mixed voices (X224). The orchestral accompaniment, for strings, may be used with either version, and is available on hire.

sa - cred sign? But where-with for sa - cred sign?

(Ped.) (Man.)

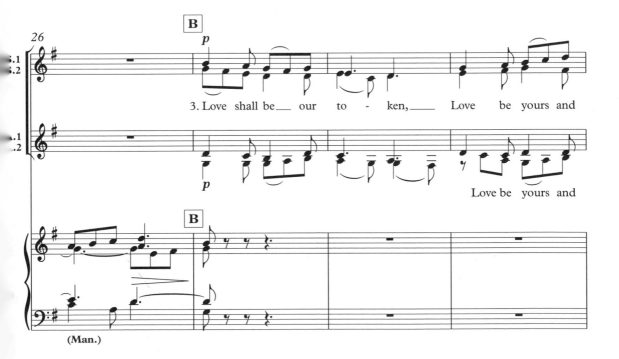

3. Love shall be __ our to - ken, __ Love be yours and

Love be yours and

(Man.)

love____ be   mine;____   Love____ to   God____ and   all_____ men,____

Love____ for   plea____ and   gift____ and   sign;____   Love____ for   plea____ and

gift_____ and   sign.

gift_____ and   sign.

(Ped.)

11. Into this world, this day did come

English trad.

HOWARD SKEMPTON
(b. 1947)

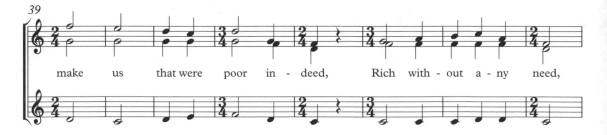

make us that were poor in - deed, Rich with - out a - ny need,

tru - ly. I pray you, be mer - ry and sing_ with me In wor -

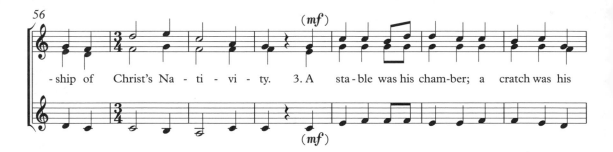

- ship of Christ's Na - ti - vi - ty. 3. A sta - ble was his cham-ber; a cratch was his

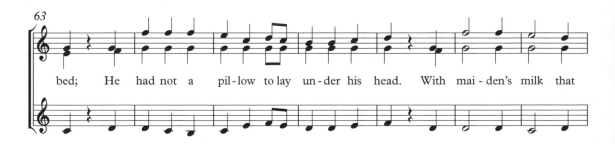

bed; He had not a pil-low to lay un-der his head. With mai - den's milk that

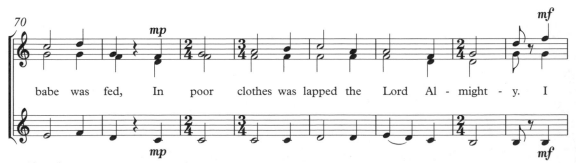

babe was fed, In poor clothes was lapped the Lord Al - might - y. I

cratch crib

pray you, be mer - ry and sing_ with me In wor - ship of Christ's Na -

(mf)

-ti - vi - ty. 4. A no - ble les - son here is us taught, To set all world

(mf)

ri - ches at naught, But pray we that we may be thi - ther

brought, where ri - ches is e - ver - last - ing - ly. I pray you, be mer -

rit.

-ry and sing_ with me In wor - ship of Christ's Na - ti - vi - ty.

October 2005

12. There is no rose

15th-cent.

ALAN SMITH
(b. 1962)

Res miranda   A wonderful thing

Paresforma   Of the same form

Gloria in excelsis Deo Glory to God on high;   *Gaudeamus* Let us rejoice

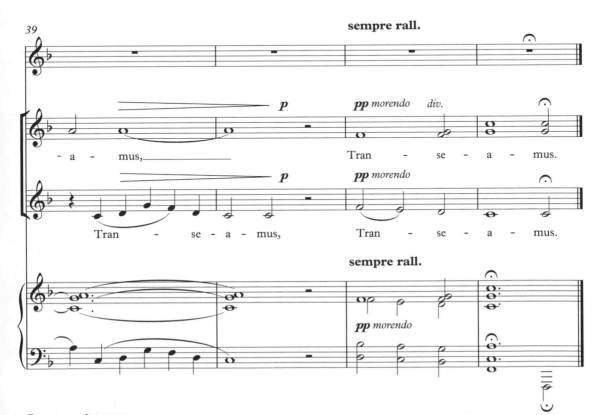

Transeamus Let us go

13. Carol of Our Lady

Medieval

CHRISTOPHER WIGGINS
(b. 1956)
op. 143 no. 3

1. To that La-dy let us sing, which that hath no
2. Such a mo-ther, La-dy dear, can we nought of

14. Remember, O thou man

Thomas Ravenscroft? (*c*.1582–1635)

JONATHAN WILLCOCKS
(b. 1953)

praise to our hea-ven-ly King, and peace to all liv-ing with a good will.

praise to our hea-ven-ly King, and peace to all liv-ing with a good will.

3. To Beth-lem did they go, O thou

ah

ah

man,   O thou man,   To   Beth-lem did___ they go   the   shep - herds___

(ah)___   ah___

(ah)___   ah___

three,   To   Beth-lem did___ they go   to   see whereit___ was   so,   if___

___ ah___   ah

___ ah___

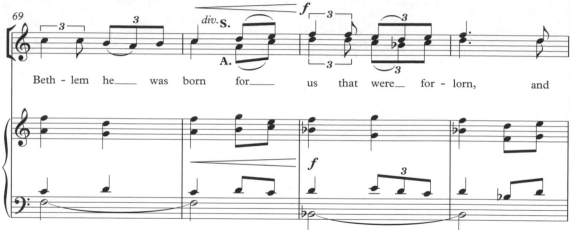

Beth - lem he__ was born for__ us that were__ for - lorn, and

there-fore took no scorn, our flesh__ to take.

5. Give thanks to God__ al - way, O thou

man, O thou man, Give thanks to God al - way most joy - ful -

- ly, Give thanks to God al - way for___ this our hap - py

day,

day,   let us all sing,

day,   let us all sing,

day, let us all sing,

let us all

sing, let us all sing and say: 'Ho - ly, ho -
let us all sing and say: 'Ho - ly, ho -
let us all sing and say: 'Ho - ly, ho -
let us all sing and say: 'Ho - ly, ho -

- ly, ho - ly!'
- ly, ho - ly!'
- ly, ho - ly!'
- ly, ho - ly!'

for Richard Vendome and the Oxford Girls' Choir

15. A Catch by the Hearth

English trad.

RODERICK WILLIAMS
(b. 1965)

* During the piece, the choir divides into 2, 3, and eventually 4 parts. Each time the choir should be split evenly.